CALIFORNIA NATIVE AMERICAN TRIBES

ACHUMAWI TRIBE

by
Mary Null Boulé

Illustrated by
Daniel Liddell

Merryant Publishers, Inc.
Vashon, WA 98070
206-463-3879

Book One in a series of twenty-seven

This series is dedicated to Virginia Harding, whose editing expertise and friendship brought this project to fruition.

Library of Congress #92-061897

ISBN: 1-877599-25-5

2

FOREWORD

Native American people of the United States are often living their lives away from major cities and away from what we call the mainstream of life. It is, then, interesting to learn of the important part these remote tribal members play in our everyday lives.

More than 60% of our foods come from the ancient Native American's diet. Farming methods of today also can be traced back to how tribal women grew crops of corn and grain. Many of our present day ideas of democracy have been taken from tribal governments. Even some 1,500 Native American words are found in our English language today.

Fur traders bought furs from tribal hunters for small amounts of money, sold them to Europeans and Asians for a great deal of money, and became rich. Using their money to buy land and to build office buildings, some traders started business corporations which are now the base of our country's economy.

There has never been enough credit given to these early Americans who took such good care of our country when it was still in their care. The time has come to realize tribal contributions to our society today and to give Native Americans not only the credit, but the respect due them.

Mary Boulé

A-frame cradle for girls; tule matting. Tubatulabal tribe.

3

GENERAL INFORMATION

Creation legends told by today's tribal people speak of how, very long ago, their creator placed them in a territory, where they became caretakers of that land and its animals. None of their ancient legends tells about the first Native Americans coming from another continent.

It is important to respect the different beliefs and theories, to learn from and seek the truth in all of them.

Villagers' tribal history lessons do not agree with the beliefs of anthropologists (scientific historians who study the habits and customs of humans).

Clues found by these scientists lead them to believe that ancient tribespeople came to North America from Asia during the Ice Age period some 20 to 35 thousand years ago. They feel these humans walked over a land strip in the Bering Straits, following animal herds who provided them with food.

Scientists' understanding of ancient people must come from studying clues; for example, tools, utensils, baskets, garbage discoveries, and stories they passed from one generation to the next.

California's Native Americans did not organize into large tribes. Instead they divided into tribelets, sometimes having as many as 250 people. Some tribelets had only one chief for each village.

From 20 to 100 people could be living in one village, which usually had several houses. In most cases, these groups of people were one family and were related to each other. From five to ten people of a family might live in one house. For instance, a mother, a father, two or three children, a grandmother, or aunt or daughter-in-law might live together.

Village members together would own the land important to them for their well-being. Their land might include oak trees with precious acorns, streams and rivers, and plants which were good to eat. Streams and rivers were especially important to a tribe's quality of life. Water drew animals to it; that meant more food for the tribe to eat. Fish were a good source of food, and traveling by boat was often easier than walking long distances. Water was needed in every part of tribal life.

Village and tribelet land was carefully guarded. Each group knew exactly where the boundaries of its land were found. Boundaries were known by landmarks such as mountains or rivers, or they might also be marked by poles planted in the ground. Some boundary lines were marked by rocks, or by objects placed there by tribal members. The size of a territory had to be large enough to supply food to every person living there.

The California tribes spoke many languages. Sometimes villages close together even had a problem understanding one another. This meant that each group had to be sure of the boundaries of other tribes around them when gathering food. It would not be wise to go against the boundaries and the customs of neighbors. The Native Americans found if they respected the boundaries of their neighbors, not so many wars had to be fought. California tribes, in spite of all their differences, were not as warlike as other tribes in our country.

Not only did the California tribes speak different languages, but their members also differed in size. Some tribes were very tall, almost six feet tall. The shortest people came from the Yuki tribe which had territory in what is now Mendocino County. They measured only about 5'2" tall. All Native Americans, regardless of size, had strong, straight black hair and dark brown eyes.

TRADE

Trading between tribes was an important part of life. Inland tribes had large animal hides that coastal tribes wanted. By trading the hides to coastal groups, inland tribes would receive fish and shells, which they in turn wanted. Coastal tribes also wanted minerals and rocks mined in the mountains by inland tribes. Obsidian rock from the northern mountains was especially wanted for arrowheads. There were, as well, several minerals, mined in the inland mountains, which could be made into the colorful body paints needed for religious ceremonies.

Southern tribes particularly wanted steatite from the Gabrielino tribe. Steatite, or soapstone, was a special metal which allowed heat to spread evenly through it. This made it a good choice to be used for cooking pots and flat frying pans. It could be carved into bowls because of its softness and could be decorated by carving designs into it. Steatite came from Catalina Island in the Coastal Gabrielino territory. Gabrielinos found steatite to be a fine trading item to offer for the acorns, deerskins, or obsidian stone they needed.

When people had no items to trade but needed something, they used small strings of shells for money. The small dentalium shells, which came from the far distant Northwest coast, had great value. Strings of dentalia usually served as money in the Northern California tribes, although some dentalia was used in the Central California tribes.

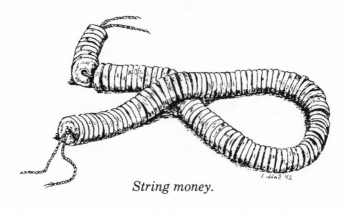

String money.

In southern California clam shells were broken and holes were bored through the center of each piece. Then the pieces were rounded and polished with sandstone and strung into strings for money. These were not thought to be as valuable as dentalia.

Strings of shell money were measured by tattoo marks on the trader's lower arm or hand.

Here is a sample of shell value:

> A house, three strings
> A fishing place, one to three strings
> Land with acorn-bearing oak trees, one to five strings

A great deal of rock and stone was traded among the tribes for making tools. Arrows had to have sharp-edged stone for tips. The best stone for arrow tips was obsidian (volcanic glass) because, when hit properly, it broke off into flakes with very sharp edges. California tribes considered obsidian to be the most valuable rock for trading.

Some tribes had craftsmen who made knives with wooden handles and obsidian blades. Often the handles were decorated with carvings. Such knives were good for trading purposes. Stone mortars and pestles, used by the women for grinding grains into flour, were good trading items.

BASKETS & POTTERY

California tribal women made beautiful baskets. The Pomo and Chumash baskets, what few are left, show us that the women of those tribes might have been some of the finest basketmakers in the world. Baskets were used for gathering and storing food, for carrying babies, and even for hauling water. In emergencies, such as flooding waters, sometimes children, women, and tribal belongings crossed the swollen rivers and streams in huge, woven baskets! Baskets were so tightly woven that not a drop of water could leak from them.

Baskets also made fine cooking pots. Very hot rocks were taken from a fire and tossed around inside baskets with a looped tree branch until food in the basket was cooked.

Most baskets were made to do a certain job, but some baskets were designed for their beauty alone and were excellent for trading. Older women of a tribe would teach young girls how to weave baskets.

Pottery was not used by many California tribes. What little there was seems to have been made by those tribes living near to the Navaho and Mohave tribes of Arizona, and it shows their style. For example, pottery of the California tribes did not have much decoration and was usually a dull red color. Designs were few and always in yellow.

Ohlone hunter wearing deerskin camouflage.

Long thin coils of clay were laid one on top the other. Then the coils were smoothed between a wooden paddle and a small stone to shape the bowl. Pottery from California Native Americans has been described as light weight and brittle (easily broken), probably because of the kind of clay soil found in California.

HUNTING & FISHING

Tribal men spent much of their time making hunting and fishing tools. Bows and arrows were built with great care, to make them shoot as accurately as possible. Carelessly made hunting weapons caused fewer animals to be killed and people then had less food to eat.

Bows made by men of Southern California tribes were made long and narrow. In the northern part of the state bows were a little shorter, thinner, and wider than those of their northern neighbors. Size and thickness of bows depended on the size trees growing in a tribe's territory. The strongest bows were wrapped with sinew, the name given to animal tendons. Sinew is strong and elastic like a rubber band.

Arrows were made in many sizes and shapes, depending on their use. For hunting larger animals, a two-piece arrow was used. The front piece of the arrow shaft was made so that it would remain in the animal, even if the back part was removed or broken off. The arrowhead, or point, was wrapped to the front piece of the shaft. This kind of arrow was also used in wars.

Young boys used a simple wooden arrow with the end sharpened to a point. With this they could hunt small animals like birds and rabbits. The older men of the tribe taught boys how to make their own arrows, how to aim properly, and how to repair broken weapons.

Tribal men spent many hours making and mending fishing nets. The string used in making nets often came from the fibers of plants. These fibers were twisted to make them strong and tough, then knotted into netting. Fences, or weirs, that had one small opening for fish, were built across streams. As the fish swam through the opening they would be caught in netting or harpooned by a waiting fisherman.

Hooks, if used at all, were cut from shells. Mostly hooks could be found when the men fished in large lakes or when catching trout in high mountain areas. Hooks were attached to heavy plant fiber string.

Dip nets, made of netting attached to branches that were bent into a circle, were used to catch fish swimming near shore. Dip nets had long handles so the fishermen could reach deep into the water.

Sometimes a mild poison was placed on the surface of shallow water. This confused the fish and caused them to float to the surface of the water, where they could be scooped up by a waiting fisherman. Not enough poison was used to make humans ill.

Not all fishing was done from the shore. California tribes used two kinds of boats when fishing. Canoes, dug out of one half a log, were useful for river fishing. These were square at each end, round on the bottom, and very heavy. Some of them were well-finished, often even having a carved seat in them.

Today we think of "balsa" as a very lightweight wood, but in Spanish, the word balsa means "raft". That is why Spanish explorers called the Native American canoes, made from tule reeds, "balsa" boats.

Balsa boats were made of bundled tule reeds and were used throughout most of California. They made into safe, lightweight boats for lake and river use. Usually the balsa canoe had a long, tightly tied bundle of tule for the boat bottom and one bundle for each side of the canoe. The front of the canoe was higher than the back. Balsa boats could be steered with a pole or with a paddle, like a raft.

Men did most of the fishing, women were in charge of gathering grasses, seeds, and acorns for food. After the food was collected, it was either eaten right away or made ready for winter storage.

Except for a few southern groups, California tribes had permanent villages where they lived most of the year. They also had food-gathering places they returned to each year to collect acorns, salt, fish, and other foods not found near their villages.

FOOD

Many different kinds of plant food grew wild in California in the days before white people arrived. Berries and other plant foods grew in the mountains. Forests offered the local tribes everything from pine nuts to animals.

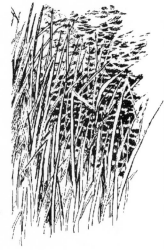

Native Americans found streams full of fish for much of the year. Inland fresh water lakes had large tule reeds growing along their shores. Tule could be eaten as food when plants were young and tender. More important, however, tule was used in making fabric for clothes and for building boats and houses. Tule was probably the most useful plant the California Native Americans found growing wild in their land.

Like all deserts, the one in southern California had little water or fish, but small animals and cactus plants made good food for the local tribes. They moved from place to place harvesting whatever was ripe. Tribal members always knew when and where to find the best food in their territory.

Acorns were the main source of food for all California tribes. Acorn flour was as important to the California Native Americans as wheat is to us today. Five types of California oak trees produced acorns that could be eaten. Those from black oak and tanbark oak seem to have been the favorite kinds.

Since some acorns tasted better than others, the tastiest ones were collected first. If harvest of the favorite acorn was poor some years, then less tasty acorns had to be eaten all winter long.

So important were acorns to California Indians that most tribes built their entire year around them. Acorn harvest marked the beginning of their calendar year. Winter was counted as so many months after acorn harvest, and summer was counted by the number of months before the next acorn harvest.

Acorn harvest ceremonies usually were the biggest events of the year. Most celebrations took place in mid-October and included dancing, feasts, games of chance, and reunions with relatives. Harvest festivals lasted for many days. They were a time of joy for everyone.

The annual acorn gathering lasted two to three weeks. Young boys climbed the oak trees to shake branches; some men used long poles to knock acorns to the ground. Women loaded the nuts into large cone-shaped burden baskets and carried them to a central place where they were put in the sun to dry.

Once the acorns were dried, the women carried them back to the tribe's permanent villages. There they lined special basket-like storage granaries with strong herbs to keep insects away, then stored the acorns inside. Granaries were placed on stilts to keep animals from getting into them and were kept beside tribal houses.

Preparing acorns for each meal was also the women's job. Shells were peeled by hitting the acorns with a stone hammer on an anvil (flat) stone. Meat from the nut was then laid on a stone mortar. A mortar was usually a large stone with a slight dip on its surface. Sometimes the mortar had a bottomless basket, called a hopper, glued to its top. This kept the acorn meat from sliding off the mortar as it was beaten.

The meat was then pounded with a long stone pestle. Acorn flour was scraped away from the hopper's sides with a soaproot fiber brush during this process.

From there the flour was put into an open-worked basket and sifted. A fine flour came through the bottom of the basket, while the larger pieces were put back in the mortar for more pounding.

The most important process came after the acorn flour was sifted. Acorn flour has a very bitter-tasting tannin in it. This bitter taste was removed by a method called leaching. Many tribes leached the flour by first scooping out a hollow in sand near water. The hollow was lined with leaves to keep the flour from washing away. A great deal of hot water was poured through the flour to wash out (leach) the bitterness. Sometimes the flour was put into a basket for the leaching process, instead of using sand and leaves.

Finally the acorn flour was ready to be cooked. To make mush, heated stones were placed in the basket with the flour. A looped tree branch or two long sticks were used to toss the hot rocks around so the basket would not burn. When the mush had boiled, it could be eaten. If the flour and water mixture was baked in an earthen oven, it became a kind of bread. Early explorers wrote that it was very tasty.

Historians have estimated that one family would eat from 1500 to 2000 pounds of acorn flour a year. One reason California native Americans did not have to plant seeds and raise crops was because there were so many acorns for them to harvest each year.

Whether they ate fish or shellfish or plant food or animal meat, nature supplied more than enough food for the Native Americans who lived in California long ago. Many believed their good fortune in having fine weather and plenty to eat came from being good to their gods.

RELIGION

Tribal members had strong beliefs in the power of spirits or gods around them. Each tribe was different, but all felt the importance of never making a spirit angry with them. For that reason a celebration to thank the spirit-gods for treating them well, took place before each food gathering and before each hunting trip, and after each food harvest.

Usually spiritual powers were thought to belong to birds or animals. Most California tribespeople felt bears were very wicked and should not be eaten. But Coyote seems to have been a kind leader who helped them if they were in trouble, even though he seems to have been a bit naughty at times. Eagle was thought to be very powerful and good to native Americans. In some tribes, Eagle was almost as powerful as Sun.

Tribes placed importance on different gods, according to the tribe's needs. Rain gods were the most important spirits to desert tribes. Weather gods, who might bring less rain or warmer temperatures, were important to northern tribes. A great many groups felt there were gods for each of the winds: North, South, East and West. The four directions were usually included in their ceremonial dances and were used as part of the decorations on baskets, pots, and even tools.

Animals were not only worshipped and believed to be spirit-gods, like Deer or Antelope, but tribal members felt there was a personal animal guardian for each one of them. If a tribal member had a deer as guardian, then that person could never kill a deer or eat deer meat.

California Native Americans believed in life after death. This made them very respectful of death and very fearful of angering a dead person. Once someone died, the name of the dead person could never again be said aloud. Since it was easy to accidentally say a name aloud, the name was usually given to a new baby. Then the dead person would not become angry.

Shamans were thought to be the keepers of religious beliefs and to have the ability to talk directly to spirit-gods. It was the job of a village shaman to cure sick people, and to speak to the gods about the needs of the people. Some tribes had several kinds of shamans in one village. One shaman did curing, one scared off evil spirits, while another took care of hunters.

Not all shamans were nice, so people greatly feared their power. However, if shamans had no luck curing sick people or did not bring good luck in hunting, the people could kill them. Most shamans were men, but in a few tribes, women were doctors.

Most California tribal myths have been lost to history because they were spoken and never written down. The legends were told and retold on winter nights around the home fires. Sadly, these were forgotten after the missionaries brought Christianity to California and moved tribal members into the missions.

A few stories still remain, however. It is thought by historians that northwest California tribes were the only ones not to have a myth on how they were created. They did not feel that the world was made and prepared for human beings. Instead, their few remaining stories usually tell of mountain peaks or rivers in their own territory.

The central California tribes had creation stories of a great flood where there was only water on earth. They tell of how man was made from a bit of mud that a turtle brought up from the bottom of the water.

Many southwest tribes believed there was a time of no sky or water. They told of two clouds appearing which finally became Sky and Earth.

Throughout California, however, all tribes had myths that told of Eagle as the leader, Coyote as chief assistant, and of less powerful spirits like Falcon or Hawk.

Costumes for religious ceremonies often imitated these animals they worshipped or feared. Much time was spent in making the dance costumes as beautiful as possible. Red woodpecker feathers were so brilliant a color they were used to decorate religious headdresses, necklaces, or belts. Deerskin clothing was fringed so shell beads could be attached to each thin strip of leather.

Eagle feathers were felt to be the most sacred of religious objects. Sometimes they were made into whole robes.

Religious feather charm.

Usually, though, the feathers were used just for decorations. All these costumes were valuable to the people of each tribe. The village chief was in charge of taking care of the costumes, and there was terrible punishment for stealing them. Clothing worn everyday was not fancy like costuming for rituals.

Willow bark skirt.

CLOTHING

Central and southern California's fine weather made regular clothes not really very important to the Native Americans. The children and men went naked most of the year, but most women wore a short apron-like skirt. These skirts were usually made in two pieces, front and back aprons, with fringes cut into the bottom edges. Often the skirt was made from the inner bark of trees, shredded and gathered on a cord. Sometimes the skirt was made from tule or grass.

In northern California and in rainy or windy weather elsewhere in the state, animal-skin blankets were worn by both men and women. They were used like a cape and wrapped around the body. Sometimes the cape was put over one shoulder and under the other arm, then tied in front. All kinds of skins were used; deer, otter, wildcat, but sea-otter fur was thought to be the best. If the skin was from a small animal, it was cut into strips and woven together into a fabric. At night the cape became a blanket to keep the person warm.

Because of the rainy weather in northern California, the women wore basket caps all the time. Women of the central and south tribes wore caps only when carrying heavy loads, where the forehead had to be used as support. Then a cap helped keep too much weight from being placed on the forehead.

Most California people went barefoot in their villages. For journeys into rough land, going to war, wood gathering, or in colder weather, the tribesmen in central and northwest California wore a one-piece soft shoe with no extra sole, which went high up on the leg.

Southern California tribespeople, however, wore sandals most of the time, wearing high, soled moccasins only when they traveled long distances or into the mountains. Leggings of skin were worn in snow, and moccasins were sometimes lined with grass for more comfort and warmth.

VILLAGE LIFE

Houses of the California tribes were made of materials found in their area. Usually they were round with domed roofs. Except for a few tribes, a house floor was dug into the earth a few feet. This was wise, for it made the home warmer in winter and cooler in summer. It also meant that less material was needed to make house walls.

Framework for the walls was made from bendable branches tied to support poles. Some frames of the houses were covered with earth and grass. Others were covered with large slabs of redwood or pine bark. Central California

Split-stick clapper, rhythm instrument. Hupa tribe.

villagers made large woven mats of tule reed to cover the tops and sides of houses. In the warmer southern area, brush and smaller pieces of bark were used for house walls.

Most California Native American villages had a building called a sweathouse, where the men could be found when they were not hunting, fishing or traveling. It was a very important place for the men, who used it rather like a clubhouse. They could sweat and then scrape themselves clean with curved ribs of deer. The sweathouse was smaller than a family house. Normally it had a center pole framework with a firepit on the ground next to the pole. When the fire was lit, some smoke was allowed to escape through a hole at the top of the roof; however, most was trapped inside the building. Smoke and heat were the main reasons for having a sweathouse. Both were believed to be a way to purify tribal members' bodies. Sweathouse walls were mainly hard-packed earth. The heat produced was not a steam heat but came from a wood-fed fire.

In the center of most villages was a large house that often had no walls, just a roof held up with poles. It was here that religious dances and rituals were held, or visitors were entertained.

Dances were enjoyed and were performed with great skill. Music, usually only rhythm instruments, accompanied the dances. For some reason California Native Americans did not use drums to create rhythms for their dances. Three different kinds of rattles were used by California tribes.

One type, split-clap sticks, created rhythm for dancing. These were usually a length of cane (a hollow stick) split in half lengthwise for about two-thirds of its length. The part still uncut was tightly wound with cord so it would not split all the way. The stick was held at the tied end in one hand and hit against the palm of the other hand to make its sound.

19

A pebble-filled moth cocoon made rhythm for shaman duties. These could range from calling on spirits to cure illnesses, to performing dances to bring rain. Probably the best sounds to beat rhythm for songs and dances came from bundles of deer hooves tied together on a stick. These rattles have a hollow, warm sound.

The only really "musical" instrument found in California was a flute made of reed that was played by blowing across the edge of one end. Melodies were not played on any of these instruments. Most North American Indians sang their songs rather than playing melodies on music instruments.

Special songs were sung for each event. There were songs for healing sick people, songs for success in hunting, war, or marriage. Women sang acorn-grinding songs and lullabies. Songs were sung in sorrow for the dead and during story-telling times. Group singing, with a leader, was the favorite kind of singing. Most songs were sung by all tribe members, but religious songs had to be sung by a special group. It was important that sacred songs not be changed through the years. If a mistake was made while singing sacred music, the singer could be punished, so only specially trained singers would sing ritual songs.

All songs were very short, some of them only 20 to 30 seconds long. They were made longer by repeating the melodies over and over, or by connecting several songs together. Songs usually told no story, just repeated words or phrases or syllables in patterns.

Song melodies used only one or two notes and harmony was never added. Perhaps that is why mission Indians, at those missions with musician priests, especially loved to sing harmony in the church choirs.

Songs and dances were good methods of passing rich tribal traditions on to the children. It was important to tribal adults that their children understand and love the tribe's heritage.

Children were truly wanted by parents in most tribes and new parents carefully watched their tiny babies day and night, to be sure they stayed warm and dry. Usually a newborn was strapped into a cradle and tied to the mother's back so she could continue to work, yet be near the baby at all times. In some tribes, older children took care of babies of cradle age during the day to give the mother time to do all her work, while grandmothers were often in charge of caring for toddlers.

Children were taught good behavior, traditions, and tribal rules from babyhood, although some tribes were stricter than others. Most of the time parents made their children obey. Young children could be lightly punished, but in many tribes those over six or seven years old were more severely punished if they did not follow the rules.

Just as children do today, Native American youngsters had childhood traditions they followed. For instance, one tribal tradition said that when a baby tooth came out, a child waited until dusk, faced the setting sun and threw the tooth to the west. There is no mention of a generous tooth fairy, however.

Tribal parents were worried that their offspring might not be strong and brave. Some tribes felt one way to make their children stronger was by forcing them to bathe in ice cold water, even in wintertime. Every once in a while, for example, Modoc children were awakened from sleep and taken to a cold lake or stream for a freezing bath.

But if freezing baths at night were hard on young Native Americans, their days were carefree and happy. Children were allowed to play all day, and some tribes felt children did not even have to come to dinner if they didn't want to. In those tribes, children could come to their houses to eat anytime of the day.

The games boys played are not too different from those played today. Swimming, hide and seek among the tule reeds, a form of tetherball with a mud ball tied to a pole, and willow-javelin throwing kept boys busy throughout the day.

Fathers made their sons small bows and arrows, so boys spent much time trying to improve their hunting skills. They practised shooting at frogs or chipmunks. The first animal any boy killed was not touched or eaten by him. Others would carry the kill home to be cooked and eaten by villagers. This tradition taught boys always to share food.

Another hunting tool for boys was a hollowed-out willow branch. This became like a modern day beanshooter, only the Native American boys shot juniper berries instead of beans. Slingshots made good hunting weapons, as well.

Girls and boys shared many games, but girls playing with each other had contests to see who could make a basket the fastest, or they played with dolls made of tule. Together, young boys and girls played a type of ring-around-the-rosie game, climbed mountains, or built mud houses.

As children grew older, the boys followed their fathers and the girls followed their mothers as the adults did their daily work. Children were not trained in the arts of hunting or basketmaking, however, until they became teenagers.

HISTORY

Spanish missionaries, led by Fray Junipero Serra, arrived in California in 1769 to build missions along the coast of California. By 1823, fifty years later, 21 missions had been founded. Almost all of them were very successful, and the Franciscan monks who ran them were proud of how many Native Americans became Christians.

However, all was not as the monks had planned it would be. Native American people had never been around the diseases European white men brought with them. As a result, they had no immunity to such illnesses as measles, small pox, or flu. Too many mission Indians died from white men's diseases.

Historians figure there were 300,000 Native Americans living in California before the missionaries came. The missions show records of 83,000 mission Indians during mission days. By the time the Mexicans took over the missions from the Spanish in 1834, only 20,000 remained alive.

The great California Gold Rush of 1849 was probably another big reason why many of the Native Americans died during that time. White men, staking their claim to tribal lands with gold upon it, thought nothing of killing any California tribesman who tried to keep and protect his territory. Fifty-thousand tribal members died from diseases, bullets, or starvation between the gold Rush Days and 1870. By 1910, only 17,000 California Indians remained.

Although the American government tried to set aside reservations (areas reserved for Native Americans), the land given to the Indians often was not good land. Worse yet, some of the land sacred to tribes, such as burial grounds, was taken over by white people and never given back.

Sadly, mission Indians, when they became Christians, forgot the proud heritage and beliefs they had followed for thousands of years. Many wonderful myths and songs they had passed from one generation to the next, on winter nights so long ago, have been lost forever.

Today some 100,000 people can claim California Native American ancestors, but few pure-blooded tribespeople remain. Our link with the Wanderers, who came from Asia so long ago, has been forever broken.

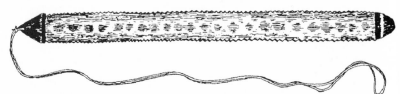

The bullroarer made a deep, loud sound when whirled above the player's head. Tipai tribe.

Villages were usually built beside a lake, stream, or river. Balsa canoes are on the shore. Tule reeds grow along the edge of the water and are drying on poles on the right side of the picture.

Women preparing food in baskets, sit on tule mats. Tule mats are being tied to the willow pole framework of a house being built by one of the men.

25

THE ACHUMAWI TRIBE

INTRODUCTION

Achumawi (Ah choo may' wee) means "river people". It was not a name the tribe called itself, but a name given to them by their tribal neighbors. White people called them the Pit River Indians because many of their permanent villages were found along the Pit River. The river's name came from large pits found on its banks, mostly dug by Achumawi hunters to trap deer.

The word Achumawi actually was the name of one of the small tribelets within the larger tribe. Anthropologists, who study the lives of ancient people, decided to give the tribelet name to the whole tribe.

THE LAND

Achumawi land ranged from Mt. Shasta (14,162 feet high) in the northwest corner, to Lassen Peak (10,466 feet high) in the southwest corner of the territory. The eastern boundary of Achumawi land was the Warner mountain range north to Goose Lake.

This land was one of many valleys and streams: there were twenty mountain peaks over 6000 feet above sea level within its boundaries. Most of the Achumawi villages along the Pit River were only about 2,000 feet above sea level, where the weather was warmer throughout the year.

Because of the great difference between high and low lands in their territory, the Achumawi found everything from swamps and lakes fed by streams, to lava-flow areas there. Each elevation had its own plants and animals that provided food for the tribe.

Even the lava-flow land was very useful to the tribe, although it was a place of only hardened lava rock. Achumawis found this region to be a good hunting place for small animals, such as groundhogs. There were fine hiding places there, as well, when enemies invaded the tribe's land. Later, during the gold rush, tribal members used this region as a shelter to hide from white men.

Higher lands were covered with fir and pine trees. The tribespeople kept ground under the trees clear by setting fires to it. Native Americans knew burning would cause plants to produce more seeds. More seeds then produced more plants, making more food for them. Burning took place on meadows and grassland, as well, for the Achumawi also used fire to drive animals into traps and to collect grasshoppers. Sometimes fire was used to fight a war.

War was not something that happened often, however. The only tribe giving Achumawi people any trouble was the Modoc tribe. Modocs would sometimes raid Achumawi territory to capture them for use as slaves. Rather than fight back, the Achumawi usually hid until Modoc raiders left for home. They were peaceable people at heart.

Several large swamplands, many of them near the center of the territory, provided more than food. Most important to the tribe, tule was found there. Tule was a tall (5-9 feet), strong reed plant. It supplied the tribe with material for every part of their daily lives.

Tule reeds were woven into mats, then the mats became house walls, mattresses, seat pads, or coverings for storage during rainy weather. The fiber of the plant was twisted into all sizes of string and cord and was woven into shoes. Men bundled it together to make canoes. Women shredded the plant's stalk to make fabric for clothing. New sprouts of the plant could even be eaten.

Achumawi land also included a treeless, dry area. But even it was not useless. In the fall, this land became a gathering place for antelope, jack rabbits, and the sage grouse, making it a splendid hunting ground for getting meat for the long winter ahead.

Winters in Achumawi territory were very cold. Deep snow covered the land every winter. Because of the cold, a great deal of fuel was needed to keep the people warm. For heat, villagers burned sagebrush, dried juniper branches, and pine trees knocked down by the wind. Without the wind's help the Native Americans might have been quite cold, for they had no tools with which to cut down trees.

Juniper trees were very important to the Achumawi. The trees were called "cedar" by the tribe. "Cedar" bark helped keep homes warm. It also kept them warm on trips. A tightly wrapped "rope" of "cedar" bark was lit at one end before a journey and carried by hunters and travelers as a slow-burning match, so that a fire could be started without using a fire drill.

Juniper bark was shredded into a fabric for women's skirts. Snowshoes used in winter hunting were often made of juniper wood. Drills for fire starters usually came from juniper wood. To start a fire, drill sticks were rapidly twirled in a small, shallow dent of a piece of sagebrush. Juniper berries were used as medicine. And juniper, along with pine, could be carved into dugout canoes.

THE VILLAGE

The Achumawi were divided into small groups we now call tribelets. Tribelets lived in villages, owning their land and governing themselves. Each tribelet took care of all its own people's needs. They spoke almost the same language as their neighbors, but each tribelet had its own special way of talking.

Big houses, often 15 feet square, were made from wood cut from trees that were knocked down by nature. The Achumawi had no stone axes or other tools to cut down trees. They did have ways of raising house poles and crossbeams to frame the sides and tops of their houses, however. The men would split logs into slabs to cover the house framework, using chisels made of antlers and hammers, or mauls made of stone. Wild grasses were used for thatching the roofs, which were then covered with dirt.

The floor of an Achumawi house was dug a few feet into the ground. A central smoke hole in the roof had a rope-like ladder that led to it. This served as a door to the house for adults. Children usually used a tunneled drafthole in the side of the house to go in and out.

VILLAGE LIFE

Each village was led by a chief, but there is no record of how a chief was chosen or what this leader's duties were.

Villagers were all related to each other in some way. Personal names were not used when speaking to someone. Instead of using names, people would be called by the relation they were to the speaker. For instance, if a girl wished to call to an aunt she just would say, "Aunt!"

Nicknames were given to friends, and strangers were called by the names of their villages or tribes. It was an insult to call people by their real names. That may seem strange to us, but it might have actually brought tribal members closer together by reminding them of how they were related to people in their village.

House made of brush and branches; the floor was dug into the ground a few feet, making the roof the only part showing above ground.

When couples married, their families exchanged presents. Rather than giving presents to keep the families friendly toward each other, the tribelets looked upon these gifts as "payment" for including the young people in the in-laws' family.

Achumawi parents taught their children that being rich was not important. It was much more important to be well-liked. Respect for being popular came before respect for how much a person owned.

There was no ritual or ceremony when a villager died. In fact, everyone had such fear of a dead body that it was quickly cremated (burned). Close relatives shaved off their hair and covered their heads with pitch, a sticky liquid from trees. A widow even wore necklaces made of pitch. Everything belonging to the dead person was burned, and the dead relative was forgotten as soon as possible.

If a chief died, however, the villagers and visitors from nearby tribelets cried and wailed outside the earth-lodge where he lay for one night. Then the body was burned.

All knew they were forbidden to speak aloud the name of the dead person. All thought that the soul of the dead person had gone to the western mountains. What they did not know — and would not ask — is what happened to souls of the dead in the mountains. They felt a soul might not want to go alone to the mountains, so it might return to get a loved one to go with it. Each relative still alive was afraid of being the one chosen to go with a dead person.

Along with death fears, Achumawi people feared bears. Bears were thought to be supernatural. Beavers were felt to be supernatural, too, but it was thought they brought good luck in gambling. Supernatural animals were very much a part of their beliefs.

While the myths of other tribes were mostly serious ones about how the world was begun, the Achumawis myths were about the funny things they said had happened long ago. Older villagers told these humorous stories in wintertime when all would huddle together for warmth in earth-lodges. As snow blew outside, people would lie down on the floor amidst smoke from the roaring fire and listen to stories. Tellers made up stories as they talked. Many stories were about Coyote and his adventures and tricks. It was like going to a movie in a theater.

RELIGION AND BELIEFS

The Achumawi may not have had religious myths like their neighboring tribes, but they still believed in a "mystic guardian spirit." It was thought that anyone could have a guardian, but people could also lose their spirits if the spirits were made angry. To have a guardian-spirit meant a person had supernatural power. It was thought a guardian made men into good hunters and brave warriors.

A shaman was the village doctor and spiritual leader. Shamans were believed to have spirits much more powerful than other villagers. Because of this power, the shaman's job was to reach out to the spirits of others in times of sickness, or when death was close.

When a shaman visited a sick person, the patient would lie down with the head facing east (because light first comes from the east each morning). Songs were sung as a way of attracting the guardian spirit of the shaman. Then the shaman began speaking in a loud voice to get the spirit's attention. It was the duty of a shaman's spirit to find the evil which was making someone sick and to make the evil go away.

Medicine used by curing shamans came from plants all over Achumawi territory, much of it from trees, herbs and moss. In all, 21 plants were believed to have had curing power. Some of the 21 plants were sagebrush, manzanita, bark of the hazelwood tree, lilies and black moss. Pine sap as well as juniper berries, were often used as medicine. Today many people are again discovering those herbal medicines used so long ago by village shamans.

When someone suffered a bad accident, people knew a shaman probably could not heal the victim, but prayers said by shamans were much like our prayers of help today. They made people feel better.

Shamans in the Achumawi tribe did not inherit their jobs from fathers or uncles, as in most other California tribes. In this tribe, elders picked likely young men or women to be shamans and then trained them. It was not a job most people really wanted to do because it could be dangerous. For instance, a shaman could be killed for not showing enough power. Shamans of another village were often asked to kill those shamans thought to be bad or unsuccessful; unhappy villagers were afraid to kill their own spiritual doctor, or shaman.

CLOTHING

Warm clothes were needed in the high northern territory, so animal skins were an important part of Achumawi clothing. Plenty of deer were to be found throughout their territory. Deerskin was tanned with deer brains by the women and made into caps, capes, robes, skirts, shirts, belts, leggings, moccasins, and dresses.

Badger skins were made into caps, capes, and moccasins. Bears were hunted for their hides and meat. The hide (skin) of elk was made into shields to be worn as protection in times of war. Antelope skins also made fine caps, shirts, and blankets. Beaver skins were very warm to wear, and beaver meat was good to eat. Best of all, beaver was thought to bring good luck in games of chance, so it was special to tribespeople.

Coyotes were hunted for food, clothing, arrow quivers,and blankets, even though they were thought to be supernatural. Actually, all animals hunted for clothing were eaten except for the tiny hummingbird. Its feathers decorated many special pieces of clothing because they were so bright in color, but the bird was far too tiny to provide food. Not only did birds give feathers for decorations, one bird, the coot, was a large enough bird that its skin could be made into warm mittens!

Not only animal hides and fur were used for clothing, however. Tule, important for so many of the tribal needs, was also valuable for clothing fabric. It was shredded into a soft fabric, which could be used for making warm capes and cloaks. Women wove the strong tule fiber into sturdy caps and shoes.

Colored minerals could easily be found throughout Achumawi land. Colors of yellow, blue, white, black, and red were used to dye clothing. Many colors came from roots and plants growing in their territory. Soot and charcoal from cooking fires could be made into fine black paint. Dyes were used in decorating arrows, bows, and people (body paints), as well as for clothing.

Woman's skirt; made of milkweed fibers.

FOOD

Lakes and streams gave the tribespeople plenty of food. Some 50 miles of salmon streams and 150 miles of streams full of bass, catfish, and trout kept them well supplied with fish. It was lucky there was so much food because the winters were long and cold. Much food had to be prepared for storage so

Native Americans did not have to venture out into the harsh winter weather to search for it.

Grasshoppers tasted good to the Achumawi people. Sometimes there were so many grasshoppers, tribal members circled a field with fire which roasted the grasshoppers as it trapped them. The roasted insects were then put in sacks made from vegetable fibers and stored to be eaten during the winter.

Epos, a wild root of today's parsley, grew in grassland areas. The carrot-like roots served as an important part of the Achumawi diet, especially since they could be dried and stored for winter food. Tiger lily bulbs and wild onions were dug up and eaten fresh or dried for seasonings. Mustard seed, and salt from saltbush leaves, also seasoned food. Sunflower seeds, clover, and thistle were eaten in early spring while they were still tender and tasty.

Forest land furnished tribal members with wild berries like currants, huckleberries, gooseberries, elderberries, and salmon berries. Piñon (pine) nuts, digger pine nuts, and sugar pine nuts all made good food. Sugar-pine sap was used as we use maple sugar today.

There were some foods Native Americans enjoyed eating in those days which we would not think of eating today, even though they are nutritious and tasty. Underground wasps' nests, angle worms, the larvae (eggs) of ants, bees, hornets, crickets, grasshoppers, and caterpillars were all considered treats in tribal days.

Groves of oak trees grew on both sides of the Pit River. Oak trees meant acorns with which to make mush and bread. Read about how the acorn flour was prepared on page 12 in the first chapter of this book.

Ducks, geese, and swans made good food, as did their eggs. The sage grouse was a very tasty bird and a favorite food of the Achumawi people. The grouse were caught by snares, shot with arrows, or driven into nets each autumn.

However, in addition to autumn grouse hunting, there was another time of the year when the birds could easily be caught. Each spring the male birds performed their mating dance to attract female mates. During the dance they were so busy, they did not notice hunters. Many sage grouse were caught this way.

Antelope, bear, elk, and mountain sheep were found in the higher mountains. Deer was easily found in most areas of Achumawi territory and was probably the main meat eaten. Small animals like rabbits, chipmunk, gopher, turtles, rats, and beaver made body-warming food in the winter. Mountain lions, wildcats, and many more animals were in plentiful supply for Achumawi hunters.

Achumawi bow made of yew and decorated. This style bow has been copied by championship archers today.

Obsidian hide scraper – used to remove hair from animals hides.

HUNTING AND FISHING

Yew trees, which liked moist weather, grew in the lower western area of Achumawi territory. Yew wood was highly prized by the tribal hunters. They believed yew wood made into the best bows. Most Achumawi bows were made from yew, mahogany, or juniper wood, and wound with sinew to make them strong. Arrow shafts could be made from wild rosewood, cane, or willow. The antlers of antelope were used as wrenches for straightening out arrow shafts. Antelope and deerskin quivers held finished arrows.

Arrow points were most often chipped from obsidian, a volcanic glass. Because of the many volcanoes in their area, Achumawi had as much obsidian for arrowheads, spearheads, knives, and skin scrapers as they needed.

Sharp arrowheads easily killed animals, but sometimes arrowheads were dipped in rattlesnake venom to make sure an animal would be killed.

Obsidian stone was the most desired stone in California, and most other tribes thought anyone who owned obsidian was rich, indeed. However, since the Achumawi people had no real need to trade and had no interest in being rich, they probably did not use obsidian much as a trading item.

Another volcanic rock the tribe found useful was pumice stone, using it much as we use sandpaper today. Hunters spent long hours rubbing pumice on arrow shafts to smooth them and make them evenly rounded so they would fly in a straight line toward the hunter's target.

Fine hunting weapons, like sharp arrowheads and sturdy, well-designed bows, made hunting easier. The wide and rather flat bow made by this tribe is still imitated by archers today.

In autumn, antelope were hunted in the sagebrush areas. Smaller game, like jackrabbits and sage hens, were shot with arrows, snared, or driven into nets during the fall hunting season.

The Achumawi men wove fishing nets from cord made of long fibers of the milkweed plant. They used many kinds of nets to catch fish. Dip nets had netting that was attached to a small branch bent into a circle. A handle was attached to the circular branch so fish caught in the net could be scooped out of the water.

Another type of net, called a gill net, was a flat piece of netting put into the water in a straight up and down position with floats tied to the top of the netting. Heads of fish could go through the netting, but not their bodies. When the fish tried to back out their gills would become caught in the netting cord.

A seine net was also used to trap fish. This large net also

had floats to keep it hanging down in water and could be pulled together by its edges trapping many fish inside. It was then pulled ashore by fishermen.

Salmon were caught as they returned to the streams to lay eggs. Bass, trout, catfish, eels, and more were caught in fishing nets placed in smaller streams.

BASKETS

No food preparation could have been done by tribal women without baskets. Willow branches and grasses from the wet-meadow areas were the usual materials collected for basketmaking. All sizes of twined baskets, from the large storage basket to finely made food baskets, were woven by the women and girls. Maidenhair fern, pine roots, and redbud bark were used for basket decoration.

TODAY

Today the Achumawi tribe, and its close neighbor, the Atsugewi (Ah sue gay' wee) tribe, together form one of the largest Native American groups in California. Women still gather epos and other wild plants. Tule is still woven into mats for home use. Basketry is still done and sold as folk art.

In 1970, there were still shamans performing rituals to remove "poisons" from sick people. For although the tribespeople now prefer a present-day doctor, they often cannot afford to go to one. Even though they have learned the shaman has no real power, it helps ease the sick person's mind to visit one.

Through all the troubles California Native Americans have had finding a place in our fast-moving life today, the Pit River Indians still work to regain forestland their ancestors once owned. They have enough people in their ancient territory to serve as a strong voice in standing up for their rights as Indians and American citizens.

ACHUMAWI TRIBE OUTLINE

I. Introduction
   A. Meaning of tribal name
   B. Meaning of river's name, today
II. The land
   A. Achumawi territory
   B. Description of the different elevations of land
   C. Lava-flow land
   D. Burning of fields
   E. Swamplands and tule
      1. Uses of tule reeds
   F. Juniper trees and their uses
      1. Bark
      2. Rope of slow-burning match
      3. Fabric and snowshoes
      4. Canoes
III. The village
   A. Tribelets and land
   B. Wooden houses
IV. Village life
   A. Nicknames
   B. Marriages
   C. Importance of being popular
   D. Death
      1. Beliefs
      2. Chief's death
   E. Myths
V. Religion and beliefs
   A. Mystic guardian-spirit
   B. Shamans
      1. Curing
      2. Herbal medicines
      3. How shamans are chosen

GLOSSARY

AWL: a sharp, pointed tool used for making small holes in leather or wood

CEREMONY: a meeting of people to perform formal rituals for a special reason; like an awards ceremony to hand out trophies to those who earned honors

CHERT: rock which can be chipped off, or flaked, into pieces with sharp edges

COILED: a way of weaving baskets which looks like the basket is made of rope coils woven together

DIAMETER: the length of a straight line through the center of a circle

DOWN: soft, fluffy feathers

DROUGHT: a long period of time without water

DWELLING: a building where people live

FLETCHING: attaching feathers to the back end of an arrow to make the arrow travel in a straight line

GILL NET: a flat net hanging vertically in water to catch fish by their heads and gills

GRANARIES: basket-type storehouses for grains and nuts

HERITAGE: something passed down to people from their long-ago relatives

LEACHING: washing away a bitter taste by pouring water through foods like acorn meal

MORTAR: flat surface of wood or stone used for the grinding of grains or herbs with a pestle

PARCHING:	to toast or shrivel with dry heat
PESTLE:	a small stone club used to mash, pound, or grind in a mortar
PINOLE:	flour made from ground corn
INDIAN RESERVATION:	land set aside for Native Americans by the United States government
RITUAL:	a ceremony that is always performed the same way
SEINE NET:	a net which hangs vertically in the water, encircling and trapping fish when it is pulled together
SHAMAN:	tribal religious men or women who use magic to cure illness and speak to spirit-gods
SINEW:	stretchy animal tendons
STEATITE:	a soft stone (soapstone) mined on Catalina Island by the Gabrielino tribe; used for cooking pots and bowls
TABOO:	something a person is forbidden to do
TERRITORY:	land owned by someone or by a group of people
TRADITION:	the handing down of customs, rituals, and belief, by word of mouth or example, from generation to generation
TREE PITCH:	a sticky substance found on evergreen tree bark
TWINING:	a method of weaving baskets by twisting fibers, rather than coiling them around a support fiber

NATIVE AMERICAN WORDS
WE KNOW AND USE

PLANTS AND TREES
hickory
pecan
yucca
mesquite
saguaro

ANIMALS
caribou
chipmunk
cougar
jaguar
opossum
moose

STATES
Dakota – friend
Ohio – good river
Minnesota – waters that
    reflect the sky
Oregon – beautiful water
Nebraska – flat water
Arizona
Texas

FOODS
avocado
hominy
maize (corn)
persimmon
tapioca
succotash

GEOGRAPHY
bayou – marshy body of
    water
savannah – grassy plain
pasadena – valley

WEATHER
blizzard
Chinook (warm, dry wind)

FURNITURE
hammock

HOUSE
wigwam
wickiup
tepee
igloo

INVENTIONS
toboggan

BOATS
canoe
kayak

OTHER WORDS
caucus – group meeting
mugwump – loner politician
squaw – woman
papoose – baby

CLOTHING
moccasin
parka
mukluk – slipper
poncho

BIBLIOGRAPHY

Cressman, L. S. *Prehistory of the Far West.* Salt Lake City, Utah: University of Utah Press, 1977.

Heizer, Robert F., volume editor. *Handbook of North American Indians; California, volume 8.* Washington, D.C.: Smithsonian Institute, 1978.

Heizer, Robert F. and Elsasser, Albert B. *The Natural World of the California Indians.* Berkeley and Los Angeles, CA; London, England: University of California Press, 1980.

Heizer, Robert F. and Whipple, M.A.. *The California Indians.* Berkeley and Los Angeles, CA; London, England: University of California Press, 1971.

Heuser, Iva. *California Indians.* PO Box 352, Camino, CA 95709: Sierra Media Systems, 1977.

Macfarlen, Allen and Paulette. *Handbook of American Indian Games.* 31 E. 2nd Street, Mineola, N.Y. 11501: Dover Publications, 1985.

Murphey, Edith Van Allen. *Indian Uses of Native Plants.* 603 W. Perkins Street, Ukiah, CA 95482: Mendocino County Historical Society, © renewal, 1987.

National Geographic Society. *The World of American Indians.* Washington, DC: National Geographic Society reprint, 1989.

Tunis, Edwin. *Indians.* 2231 West 110th Street, Cleveland, OH: The World Publishing Company, 1959.

Weatherford, Jack. *Native Roots.* 201 E. 50th., New York, N.Y.: Crown Publishers, Inc. 1991.

Credits:
Island Industries, Vashon Island, Washington 98070
Dona McAdam, Mac on the Hill, Seattle, Washington 98109

Acknowledgements:
Richard Buchen, Research Librarian, Braun Library,
Southwest Museum
Special thanks